From My Heart to Yours

*Devotional and Prayers from the
Heart of God to the People of God*

Yvonne D. Quarles

Sandra
My Beautiful Queen Sister
May God Bless you with
good health, great wealth,
peace, grace & favor.
Love you!
Yvonne D. Quarles

Yvonne D. Quarles

GHG City Press, Charlotte, NC

ISBN: 978-1-7342113-0-6

Scripture taken from The Holy Bible, New King James Version, Copyright © 1982 by Thomas Nelson.

Yvonne D. Quarles

frommyhearttoyours.yq@gmail.com

Edited by Tiphane Pate

tiphane.deas@gmail.com

Acknowledgements / Dedication

I want to first acknowledge Jesus Christ, who is Lord and Savior of my life. Without Him, I could do nothing. I would like to dedicate this book to my mother, son, grandchildren, family and friends, the Body of Christ and to the world.

Mom, you have seen the gift of words that God blessed me with since I was just a little girl making you cards and you never stopped pushing me to share it with the world. Mom and Dad, you are absolutely amazing parents and I'm grateful to God for you. For all of this, I say thank you and I love you.

Timothy, my son. My one and only. You bring my heart joy when I think about you. You will always have my unconditional love and support. I pray that you will always know the love of the Father and walk in it.

Ryan and Raylon, my wonderful grandchildren, this book is for you. You have a voice. You are both generals for your generation with an inheritance that is great. You have gifts, abilities, and wisdom beyond your years. My prayer is that you would give yourself away, use it all for Jesus, let Him get the glory and let Him bless you. I love you so and thank God for you.

To my family and friends, thank you for your constant love, support, and encouragement. You came alongside me and lifted up my arms. You encouraged me to trust the Lord's work in me and give it everything I had, and this is a product of that. Thank you and I love you.

To Annette Jones, my forever best friend for many years. You are my biggest supporter and cheerleader. I am so grateful to God for you.

Only He can reveal how much I love you. My life has been so blessed by having you in it. I so love and appreciate you!

Baneshia Wyatt, you gave me a safe place to grow until I became strong enough to come into my own, and you have never changed your commitment of friendship and love. Thank you. I love you!

Leolene Hinds, you kept the vision before me constantly, reminding me that people are waiting. Thank you for surrounding me with prayer and love and keeping my feet to the fire until it was done. I love you!

Alma Miller, thank you for being my saving grace and being right there for me when I needed you the most. I love you!

To the Body of Christ and to the world: This has been a labor of love and it is my gift to you from the heart of Jesus Christ, our Lord. I have enjoyed every moment of spending time with the Lord and listening to Him, writing down what He said to give to you from His heart for your encouragement, liberty and freedom. Through these anointed devotionals and prayers, may you find hope, strength, deliverance, peace, joy, and love from the Heart of God to yours!

I love you!

Special Thanks to Integrative Ink, Tiphane Pate, Hiawatha Hemphill, Patrice Covington-Green, Rated Roz Photography, BrandNiquely You Inc and everyone who played a role in making this devotional a reality.

Devotions and Prayers...
From My Heart to Yours

Testimonials

I am grateful that I have had the opportunity to walk through this devotional journey. No matter what is going on, each day that I read them I find hope, strength, joy, and peace. I have become more loving, more faithful, more giving because of the words I have found in these pages. I thank God each day that I read them because they breathe the breath of life in me.

~ *Talibah Petway, Raleigh, NC*

My dear sister, I have been silent so the woman of God could minister unto me. The enemy has tried me on every side, level, and approach but the Word has stood firm to let me know and understand to be still, know that I serve a God who will never leave me, deceive me, nor forsake me, and loves me unconditionally...Glory! Thank you for being obedient and standing on the wall telling all, Jesus is real and salvation is free to those who choose to believe! Love you more each and every day. Be blessed!

The Goliath moments in this life will come. The messages from My Heart to Yours give comfort and hope that you are not alone on this journey. Your Exodus experience is only a prayer away. My dearest sister in Christ Jesus, thank you for your guidance and Word from above!

~ *Sheila Haynes, Charlotte, NC*

"It shall come to pass in that day that his burden will be taken away from your shoulder, and his yoke from your neck, and the yoke will be destroyed because of the anointing oil."
~ Isaiah 10:27 NKJV

DEVOTIONAL

Day 1

The anointing destroys the yoke!

It doesn't matter what it is that has us yoked and bound: the yoke of sickness and disease, division and hate, depression and oppression, fear and doubt, poverty and lack. It doesn't even matter how long the yokes or bondages have been in place. The Lord gives us strength when we partner with Him in The Holy Spirit to destroy them. The Lord is all-powerful, and all knowing. His anointing destroys the hold of any and every kind of bondage, and as a result, all chains are broken in His presence.

He restores marriages and relationships. He is concerned about every problem that concerns us, and He addresses them head on. The anointing of The Holy Spirit removes the burden and destroys the yoke of any person or thing that has attached itself to us. He now replaces it with peace and power. The Lord, He is Lord. He is the Lover of our souls, our Way Maker, our Caretaker, and the Lifter of our heads. He hears our cries and answers our prayers. There is no one like the Lord, and He is with us every day to take the burden from our shoulders, and the yoke from our neck.

PRAYER

Heavenly Father,

Thank You for another blessed day that You have allowed us to see. Thank You, Lord, for a fresh touch of Your anointing, and we ask You to rekindle the fire within us to serve and obey You better. Fill us to overflowing. We know with the anointing of the Holy Spirit, He will destroy every yoke of bondage and all chains will be broken. We pray the eyes of our understanding be enlightened that You may show us the yokes that need to be broken in our lives and give us an obedient heart and mind to act on what You show us, so we can have liberty to serve You freely. We are determined to obey the Word, keep a smile on our faces and joy in our hearts, which confuses the devil, and has him running in terror. We are blessed beyond measure with Your light and Your love when the anointing of the Holy Spirit rests upon us. We thank You and give You glory, honor, and praise for taking away the burden from our shoulders, and the yoke from our necks where we can find real peace and rest which only comes from You. We stand and confidently trust that You and Your Word will come through for us. We thank You for these and all things in Jesus Christ's name. Amen!

Always know that God loves you, and I do, too!

"That his burden will be taken away from your shoulder…"

God's Word...

"And His name, through faith in His name, has made this man strong, whom you see and know. Yes, the faith which comes through Him has given him this perfect soundness in the presence of you all."
~ Acts 3:16 NKJV

DEVOTIONAL

Day 2

Faith in Christ makes us strong!

To build up natural muscles, you normally exercise using some form of weight for resistance, believing that with consistency you will see a change. To build up spiritual muscles, the process is the same. The resistance we use comes from the weight of walking by faith and not by sight, resisting the temptation to fear and doubt. We train by lifting the Word in our minds above our natural thoughts, speaking it from our mouths and pushing it against the situation that is contrary to what we want. If we are consistent in our spiritual training, the initial resistance in our natural mind to what the Word of God says will have to change. We have to build up a resistance to everything that is contrary to that for which we believe God.

By applying the Word of God consistently over our circumstances and situations, we begin to receive the strength and ability to truly trust in God to change everything in our lives to which we apply the Word. When we trust and believe, putting faith in Jesus Christ's name only, He will give us perfect soundness of body in healing and wholeness. Nothing missing, nothing broken. Jesus Christ is the same yesterday, today, and forever. He changes not. His desire is to heal us completely from the inside out. Heal our body, heal our mind, heal our emotions, and our finances. There is nothing impossible for God, if we trust and believe in His Word.

PRAYER

Heavenly Father,

Thank You for another blessed day that You have allowed us to see. Lord, we come boldly before the throne of grace, thanking You in advance for our healing. We believe Your Word that says by Your stripes, we are healed: healed in our bodies, healed in our souls (mind, will, and emotions), and healed in our finances. You died so we would be complete and have no lack. You said that You came so we would have life and have it more abundantly, until it overflows onto others. We thank You that there's nothing missing and nothing broken, and we only receive healing and wholeness freely from You, Lord, because we put our belief, faith and trust in You alone. We give You glory, honor, and praise for paving the way, for restoration, for the turn around, and for giving us healing, hope, strength, comfort, joy, peace, and a sound mind. We thank You for Your unconditional, unrelenting, and everlasting love that is a blood covenant and can't be broken. We stand and confidently trust that You and Your Word will come through for us. We thank You for these and all things in Jesus Christ's name. Amen!

Always know that God loves you, and I do, too!

God's Word...

"...through faith in His name, has made this man strong..."

"And Jesus said to them, "I am the bread of life. He who comes to Me shall never hunger, and he who believes in Me shall never thirst." ~ John 6:35 NKJV

DEVOTIONAL
Day 3

Jesus is our sustaining meal!

Have you ever had a delicious meal and immediately felt satisfied? You couldn't think of another thing that you could possibly want at that time. Well, Jesus Christ is the bread of life and He has left us a daily portion of a sustaining meal that totally satisfies us spiritually. Like the manna that God fed the Israelites in the wilderness, He only gives us enough for the day that we are in. He wants that connection to us every day, to form and develop an intimate relationship, and reduce our independence from Him. If we come to the Lord, we will never hunger, and if we believe in Him, we will never thirst because everything we will need for each day is found in the Word.

However, just as we need our natural meals each day to keep us strong and in good health, we need our spiritual meals in the same way. We know that "without faith it is impossible to please Him, for he who comes to God must believe that He is, and that He is a rewarder of those who diligently seek Him" (Hebrews 11:6). We must come, eat, drink, believe, and be rewarded daily. Faith is spiritual food for the hungry soul, and each meal is filled with precious, powerful promises. We get it when we take in the Word of God every day. Through it, He gives our words supernatural power, He strengthens our stand against every storm, and He reveals to us anything and anyone who will do us evil or harm. He goes before us and makes crooked places straight, and rough places smooth; He orders our steps around the traps the enemy has set for us. And all He asks for in return is that we spend time with Him so we can learn and know his character, and He can fill us with the love He has for us.

PRAYER

Heavenly Father,

Thank You for another blessed day that You have allowed us to see. We must confess that Jesus Christ is Lord, and that in the Word of God, we possess the best love story ever written. You feed us with heavenly food from above that will sustain us on earth and will carry us into everlasting life. Lord, we thank You that the time that we sit and dine with You has dividends that will pay off for years to come. Lord, everything You daily reveal to us prepares us for the next thing to come. Your desire for us is never to be caught off guard, to never be found weak or weary, so that the devil will not be able to steal, kill, and destroy us. We need a steady, daily diet of the Word and of spending time with You to build ourselves up and always be alert. You said that Your sheep listen to Your voice and follow You. We know that the Word of God teaches us how to listen to You, and how to quiet the voices and chatter of others. Thank You, Lord, that You watch jealousy over us, and in You, we live in a gated community where we cannot be touched by the enemy.

We thank You that, because we are eating Your spiritual food on a regular basis, we will hunger and thirst no more and we will carry Your favor everywhere we go. Doors will be opened, and opportunities will be given, all because we took the time to sit and dine with You and follow Your directions daily. For this, we give You glory, honor, and praise! We confidently trust that You and Your Word will come through for us. We thank You for these and all things in Jesus Christ's name. Amen!

Always know that God loves you, and I do, too!

66 God's Word...

"I am the bread of life."

"Do not be deceived, God is not mocked; for whatever a man sows, that he will also reap. For he who sows to his flesh will of the flesh reap corruption, but he who sows to the Spirit will of the Spirit reap everlasting life." ~ Galatians 6:7-8 NKJV

DEVOTIONAL

Day 4

Whatever we sow, we will reap!

This is an exciting time to be in the Kingdom of God. Things are happening faster than ever before. Prayers are being answered and ways are being made as we serve the Lord day by day. You cannot sow and not reap. You cannot invest and not be blessed. You cannot connect and not inherit. We need to be in the right environment to grow, and have the right nourishments pumped into us on a regular basis. The fruit that we produce will be a direct reflection of the meal we have been eating, and our application of what we have received. The more we apply of the Word, the more opportunities we give the Lord to open up pathways and work behind the scenes to change things for us. If it's taking a little longer than you thought, don't be deceived: God is not mocked. Whatever a man, woman, boy, or girl sows, that he or she will also reap. If we sow to the flesh, of the flesh we will reap corruption, but if we sow to the Spirit, we will reap from the Spirit everlasting life. God always reminds us to choose life, choose good, choose to do right, for there is a law in place that will fulfill itself.

One of the most amazing things about the Word of God is that it reveals all of the ins and outs of life. It shares with us what we should and shouldn't do in order to be blessed, healthy, peaceful, directed, protected and everything in between. It has an answer to every situation in life, if we will take the time and study it, meditate on it, and keep it before our eyes. The very best investment we could ever make is sowing into the Kingdom of God with our time, finances, and obedience.

PRAYER

Heavenly Father,

Thank You for another blessed day that You have allowed us to see. Thank You, Lord, for giving us the inside scoop on how the Word of God works. Thank You for letting us know that if we sow to the flesh, we will reap corruption, even though it may bring temporary pleasure for a season. If we sow to the Spirit, we will reap from the Spirit everlasting life. Even though it may be painful to the flesh, we know that to get Your best, the flesh has to be crucified. Lord, help us to follow Your example, endure the cross we have to bear and help us to see the good and expected end from the beginning.

Lord, help us to understand the importance of standing on the promises of scripture so that when the enemy attacks us for the Word's sake, it's the power of the Word spoken in faith that backs him up and sends him running. Help us not to back down when things get hard, because the Kingdom of Heaven suffers violence, but the violent take it by force. Remind us that we have all the backing of Heaven surrounding us. Lord, since we know we reap what we sow, we are determined to say only what You say about us. We are the head and not the tail, above only and not beneath. We are the lender, and not the borrower. You are our Shepherd and we do not want. You anoint our head with oil. You lead us beside the still waters. You set a table before us in the presence of our enemies. We reign in victory. We are winners. We are more than conquerors through Christ Jesus, who loves us unconditionally. We thank You for these and all things in Jesus Christ's name. Amen!

Always know that God loves you, and I do, too!

"*...for whatever a man sows, that he will also reap.*"

God's Word...

The LORD has appeared of old to me, saying: 'Yes, I have loved you with an everlasting love; Therefore with lovingkindness I have drawn you.'" ~ Jeremiah 31:3 NKJV

DEVOTIONAL

Day 5

Loving kindness draws!

Let's start off by dispelling the lie that God uses sickness and disease and adverse things to chastise His children. In the natural, we would call that child abuse, and in the spirit, it would be worse. The Lord said He is God and He changes not. He is the same yesterday, today, and forever. If He used love and kindness to draw us in the beginning, wouldn't it make sense for Him to continue that since He is love? His Word tells us He is for us and not against us. He heals us from all our sickness and diseases. For us, He has a good plan and expected end. He made us the head only, and never the tail. He gives us all things that pertain to life and godliness. He robes us in His Righteousness. He calls us His beloved and He has accepted us as His very own. He saved our lives from a burning hell. He strengthens us daily and gives us victory. He is an absolutely awesome and amazing Father who takes care of all who belongs to Him. He gives us angels to surround us for our protection and to minister to us daily. The next time we are going through and the devil tells us that lie, let's talk back and tell Him what Jesus did at His resurrection, making an open show of him. We are loved with an everlasting love, and that will never change, for the Lover of our soul does not change. His love remains the same for us. All His promises are yes and amen.

PRAYER

Heavenly Father,

We thank You for another day that You have allowed us to see. We thank You for being the Lover of our soul, the healer of our hearts, and the God who changes not. You love us with an everlasting love that no devil in hell or on earth can do anything about. You drew us with Your loving kindness, and since You are love, your character doesn't possess anything else. Your tender mercies are new every morning. You watch jealously over us. Thank You for protecting us from dangers seen and unseen, and for stopping them in their tracks by our surrounding angels. We gather early at the feet of Your throne to worship You alone. You have taught us that the devil is so vain that when we start worshipping you and resist him, he has to flee. You are a good, good Father on whom we can depend to deliver us. We thank You for sealing us with Your Holy Spirit of Promise, which is the evidence that we belong to You. With lovingkindness You have drawn us, and we thank You that every day you have constantly remained the same towards us. We stand and confidently trust that You and Your Word will come through for us. We thank You for these and all things in Jesus Christ's name. Amen!

Always know that God loves you, and I do, too!

God's Word...

"Yes, I have loved you with an everlasting love."

"Therefore My Father loves Me, because I lay down My life that I may take it again. No one takes it from Me, but I lay it down of Myself. I have power to lay it down, and I have power to take it again. This command I have received from My Father." ~ *John 10:17-18 NKJV*

DEVOTIONAL
Day 6

Real love lays down its life for another!

We all have an innate desire to be loved on the deepest level, to know and be known by another. We want to be loved and we want someone to love. But have we considered what real love does? Real love lays down its life for another. It prefers the other over itself. It does for another unselfishly. It sacrifices its life to make another's life better. If You ever wanted to be loved, deeply, passionately, unselfishly, and completely without being judged in any way, let me introduce you to Jesus. Whatever you're looking for, you'll find it's all in the person of Christ Jesus: the One who loves You completely, heals You in broken places, comforts and fills a void, tenderizes a hardened heart, delivers you from yourself, and takes you to places you never dreamed of. Jesus demonstrated real love in that He willingly and freely laid down His life for You. If you were the only one who needed it, the crucifixion would still have happened. Your salvation means that much to the Lord. His desire is for your life to be better every day, in every way. No one takes His life, but He laid it down when He was crucified. He stayed on the cross because He had you on His mind.

PRAYER

Heavenly Father,

Thank You for another blessed day that You have allowed us to see. Thank You, Lord, for willingly laying Your life down for us. Help us, Lord, to walk in Your will and walk in Your ways, to be obedient to You all of our days. Thank You, Jesus, for salvation, nothing missing, broken, or lacking. Thank You for the cross. Because of Your shed blood on Calvary, we can come boldly before the throne of grace with no guilt, no shame, and no condemnation. We are now whole and complete in You. We are accepted in the Beloved. We are blood bought and blood washed, and we belong to You. We have life and life more abundantly, until it overflows in increase and surplus. Thank You for giving us all things that pertain to life and godliness. We are so grateful that when You rose up, we rose with You. We call upon Your name with assurance that You hear and will answer us if we ask anything according to Your will and do not doubt. There is no other name whereby we can be saved, set free, delivered, and given life abundantly except the precious name of Jesus Christ. We confidently trust that You and Your Word will come through for us. We thank You for these and all things in Jesus Christ's name. Amen!

Always know that God loves you, and I do, too!

"No one takes it from Me, but I lay it down of Myself."

God's Word...

"Now the man from whom the demons had departed begged Him that he might be with Him. But Jesus sent him away, saying, 'Return to your own house, and tell what great things God has done for you.' And he went his way and proclaimed throughout the whole city what great things Jesus had done for him." ~ Luke 8:38-39 NKJV

DEVOTIONAL

Day 7

How grateful are you for what the Lord has done?

We all have a gratitude meter that shows different degrees of gratefulness for what the Lord has done for us. Normally, the more you have been delivered from, the more grateful to the Lord you are. We are the ones who determine daily how grateful we are going to be. Whatever the Lord has done for us, we should publish it like a walking book, telling others about all the great things that He has done throughout our lives. Tell of His love and faithfulness and how He saved, healed, and delivered us, and how he kept us from destruction on a constant basis. As we look back over our lives, we should be able to see the Hand of God in protection mode in various ways and places. It was there before we were ever saved. We will see He has always been with us to severely restrict the scope of the enemy's activity, or things would have, should have, and could have been much worse.

PRAYER

Heavenly Father,

Thank You for another blessed day that You have allowed us to see. Lord, thank You for constraining the enemy in our lives on so many occasions and levels. We look over our book of remembrance, where we write down all the answers to prayers you have answered and ways you have delivered us. You've brought us out with a very strong hand from the enemy who thought he had destroyed and defeated us. You saved and delivered us from the flesh, the world, and the devil, which left us with a grateful praise in our hearts for You. We thank You that often times, You've protected us from ourselves and the bad choices we were making. We thank You for comforting our hearts and healing them when they had been broken or when we lost loved ones and friends that meant so much to us. You surround us with Your peace, love, joy, comfort and strength. Nobody can comfort and heal us in our deepest parts as You do.

We have a grateful heart that speaks well of You at all times. We will proclaim the Word of God and tell how it has changed our lives. We will give our testimony to those You want us to witness to. We are grateful to be a walking publication of the great things You have done for us. We thank You for being a God that changes not. We stand in awe and wonder of Your unconditional, unrelenting love and faithfulness towards us. You are a great God, and a great King above all gods. There is no one like You in all the earth, world, or universe. We stand and confidently trust that You and Your Word will come through for us. We thank You for these and all things in Jesus Christ's name. Amen!

Always know that God loves you, and I do, too!

"Return to your own house, and tell what great things God has done for you."

God's Word...

"'For with God nothing will be impossible.' Then Mary said, 'Behold the maidservant of the Lord! Let it be to me according to your word.' And the angel departed from her." ~ Luke 1:37-38 NKJV

DEVOTIONAL
Day 8

Nothing is impossible with God!

We have all been in situations that seem impossible to the naked eye; some of us are in them even now. They are those times when emotions are running high and your mind is telling you everything, except what the Word of God has to say. Or, they are the times when you're rehearsing the situation over and over in your mind, and you start saying what you're seeing. Then things begin to escalate because you start believing what you are saying. You have to come to the end of yourself and agree with the Word of God the way that Mary did. Nothing seemed to be a more impossible task than the news given to her about her life's purpose. Still, Mary trusted the Word of God given to her by the angel and she immediately agreed with what the angel said, saying, "Let it be to me according to your Word" (verse 38). And the angel departed from her because he had his marching orders from the agreement of her words.

When we agree with the Word of God and speak it aloud, even when we don't understand how He is going to deliver on His promise, we give our angels things in our lives to work on and to work out on our behalf. They will turn things around and open new doors; they will do whatever it takes to fulfill the Word of the Lord and bring to pass what we have spoken that agrees with The Word of God. The angels are mighty ones who listen to the voice of His command and who do His bidding. We have to come into agreement and into fellowship with the Lord of the Harvest for our lives to change the way Mary's did. She never looked at her circumstances. She took the Lord at His Word, and by faith trusted Him to do what He said. With God, nothing will be impossible to them that believe and trust in Him.

PRAYER

Heavenly Father,

Thank You for another blessed day that You have allowed us to see. We ask that You help us to make it a fruitful, God-ordained, and faith-filled day. Help us to walk by faith and not by sight, making up in our minds that we are going to take You at Your Word from the start. Help us to adjust our thoughts, heart, words, and eyes to stay focused on Your Word. You said that we should meditate on it day and night, so when life happens we will have the right response and make our own way prosperous. Help us to always agree with Your Word, because the angels are listening to our voice, waiting to act on our words. Words are one of the most important and powerful weapons that we have.

They can speak victory or defeat. Every time we speak, we choose to create, and we choose what we create. Create in us a clean, pure heart and renew the right spirit in us. We ask You to forgive us from all negative words that we have ever spoken, and give us a seed crop failure in that area that we have spoken negative words in. Reverse the negative words as we speak positive ones. Help us to trust You to turn things around for us. We believe that nothing is impossible when we come into agreement with You. We thank You for always being on our side; now help us to always side with The Word of God. We desire today to walk in Your ways and to obey. We are thankful for a mind and heart that agrees with You and stands on Your Word until our change comes. We stand and confidently trust that You and Your Word will come through for us. We thank You for these and all things in Jesus Christ's name. Amen!

Always know that God loves you, and I do, too!

66 God's Word...

"For with God nothing will be impossible."

DEVOTIONAL

Day 9

Are you clothed and in your right mind?

Everyone who has come to the Lord has a past made up of things that we have encountered, and spirits that were in us from which we needed deliverance. The Lord is the only one who can deliver us, and as we sit at His feet and learn of Him, He will enclose us in our right minds, which is the mind of Christ. The mind of the world that we had in the past has to be reprogrammed to do things the Lord's way. The Kingdom of God's ways are right side up and opposite of everything the world has taught us. The ways of the world are constantly changing while the Word of God is consistent and remains the same. The mind of Christ says to love; the mind of the world says to hate. The mind of Christ moves us to give; the mind of the world leads us to take. The mind of Christ aims toward peace; the mind of the world points us toward worry. The mind of Christ is victory; the world's is defeat. The Word of God is our medicine that we take every day; it heals our hearts, minds, and physical bodies no matter what state we find ourselves in. We have to choose each and every day which mind we are going to be clothed in: the mind of Christ or the mind of the world.

PRAYER

Heavenly Father,

Thank You for another blessed day that You have allowed us to see. We thank You for clothing us in our right minds as we sit at Your feet early in the morning, like Jesus did, to commune with You. We thank You for right side up Kingdom principles that put the world, the flesh and the devil in proper perspective. Open up our spiritual and natural eyes to give us the mind of Christ in every situation. We pray that the eyes of our understanding be enlightened, that we may know the hope of Your calling in Christ Jesus. Help us to learn and to apply Your Word to our lives, because that is our only saving grace. Please light up our paths and direct our footsteps to guide us in Your way everlasting. We trust You to protect us, direct us, prosper our ways, and heal our hearts, minds, and bodies. We look to You and You alone to raise us up and bring us to a place of maturity in You. Bring us to a place where we no longer desire milk in nursing, but we desire the meat of the Word to sustain us and allow us to help others. We ask You to search our hearts and minds and remove everything in us that is not like You. Please create within us a clean heart and renew a right spirit within us. Our heart's desire is to please You in a great way and to be all You have purposed for us to be. We stand in awe of Your wonderful ways. We give You glory, honor, and praise for showing us the right way to live, and for giving us a willing and obedient Spirit. We stand and confidently trust that You and Your Word will come through for us. We thank You for these and all things in Jesus Christ's name. Amen!

Always know that God loves you, and I do, too!

66 God's Word...

"...sitting at the feet of Jesus, clothed and in his right mind."

"And the LORD, He is the One who goes before you. He will be with you, He will not leave you nor forsake you; do not fear nor be dismayed." ~ Deuteronomy 31:8 NKJV

DEVOTIONAL

Day 10

The Lord will go before you!

We have many precious promises in the Word of God and one of them is that wherever you go or whatever you do, the Lord will go before you. He promises not to leave nor forsake you. Trust that the Ever-Present God is with you. The Lord is in you and for you. When you call upon the Lord, you invite Him into your situation. He goes before you and works things out on your behalf before you even get there. Doors will automatically open unto you for the places He directs you to. He will place people in your path and divinely connect you to them. The Lord is a good God and He never wants you to be dismayed or fear anything. His desire is for you to call on Him, to trust and believe that He is and that He is a rewarder of those who diligently seek Him. Trust in the Lord with all your heart, lean not to your own understanding, acknowledge Him in all your ways and He will direct your path (Proverbs 3:5-6). Know without a doubt that every decision you make when the Lord directs you will eventually get you to your divine destiny and your wealthy place in Him.

PRAYER

Heavenly Father,

Thank You for another blessed day that You have allowed us to see. We thank You for Your constant reassurance of Your loving kindness, tender mercies and for guidance for our lives. Thank You for allowing us to rest in You from all the cares that the world puts us through. Thank You that, according to Your Word, if we keep our minds on You, You will keep us in perfect peace. Many places in Your Word tell us not to fear, not to worry, and not to be afraid of anything because You are always with us. When we really trust and believe that You have our backs, the fear will disappear, and our praise will come back.

Thank You for being in a permanent blood covenant with us that cannot be broken. You said that no man can pluck the ones the Father has given You out of Your hand. For this, we thank and praise You. You are able to keep us from falling when we follow Your Word. Thank You that the Word of God is a keeper for those who want to be kept. You love us so much and so strongly, that even when we don't want to be kept, You still do not let go of us. You are an amazing Shepherd, knowing that we as your sheep always need Your help, and you are constantly drawing us. You are a very present help in the time of trouble. Your ears are open to our cry. That's why You sent us the Holy Spirit, The Helper, to help us. We stand and confidently trust that You and Your Word will come through for us. We thank You for these and all things in Jesus Christ's name. Amen!

Always know that God loves you, and I do, too!

> "He will not leave you nor forsake you; do not fear nor be dismayed."
God's Word...

"Have you not known? Have you not heard? The everlasting God, the LORD, The Creator of the ends of the earth, Neither faints nor is weary. His understanding is unsearchable." ~ Isaiah 40:28 NKJV

Day 11

Have you not heard?

Do you know the God that you serve? Do you know the character and integrity of the Creator? Do you know the one who has sent His one and only Son to purchase you, to bring back to life everything that was previously given away? He doesn't sleep nor does He slumber. His eyes move back and forth throughout the whole earth to show Himself strong and support those whose hearts are completely His. The eyes of the Lord are upon the righteous and His ears are open to their prayers. Have you not known? Have you not heard? The everlasting God, the Lord, The Creator of the ends of the earth, Neither faints nor is He weary. His understanding is unsearchable (Isaiah 40:28). The eyes of the Lord are inescapable; He misses nothing in any way. You can rest in the arms of the Lord. His love is undeniable, unconditional, and unrelenting. His covenant is an everlasting covenant that cannot be broken. He will never leave you nor forsake you. He will be the rock that keeps you stable. He gives power to the faint and strength to the weak.

PRAYER

Heavenly Father,

Thank You for another blessed day that You have allowed us to see. Who is like You, Lord? Absolutely no one. You are the Creator. You watch over us day and night, and You strengthen us for every battle. You go before us to make crooked places straight and rough places smooth. You open doors of favor and victory, and close doors of deception and defeat. You surround us with Your grace and favor as a shield. You put a guard around us on every side, so the enemy cannot penetrate us with his words or his actions. You are the lifter of our heads and the lover of our souls. You are the Great I Am, the soon coming King, the Alpha and the Omega, the Beginning and the End, You are Lord of everything. You are our shield and shelter, and You are the refuge that we run to. You neither faint nor are You ever weary. You strengthen us where we are weak and build us up where we have been torn down. You are the Good Shepherd who provides graciously for us. Your eyes are open over us and Your ears are forever open to our prayers. We thank You for hearing and answering when we call on You in faith, believing we receive what we have prayed for. We stand and confidently trust that You and Your Word will come through for us. We thank You for these and all things in Jesus Christ's name. Amen!

Always know that God loves you, and I do, too!

God's Word...

"The LORD, The Creator of the ends of the earth..."

"To grant us that we, Being delivered from the hand of our enemies, Might serve Him without fear, In holiness and righteousness before Him all the days of our life." ~ Luke 1:74-75 NKJV

DEVOTIONAL

Day 12

Deliverance is ours!

Since we are children of the Most High God, deliverance is a part of the benefits package. We are chosen and adopted into a family of royalty, set apart from the hands of our enemies. God delivers us from the enemies of sickness and disease, of lack and poverty, of oppression, depression, and suicidal tendencies. The enemies of doubt and fear, of worry and despair, of perversion and sexual sins, and captivity of our minds and wills have no claim to us. It does not matter what we need deliverance from, the Lord of Hosts with the Holy Spirit our Helper is here to assist us today for total, complete and righteous deliverance. It is His will that we live without fear or bondage. We are to serve the Lord with all of our heart, soul, and might, and offer our bodies as a living sacrifice. We are to serve Him in holiness (set apart, righteous, purified) as agents of change, Kingdom Builders before Him all the days of our lives. We can live in freedom and liberty in Him and for His glory.

PRAYER

Heavenly Father,

Thank You for another blessed day that You have allowed us to see. We thank You that Your hand of deliverance reaches deep into a sinful heart and into every situation to bring liberty and freedom to us. We know that salvation is immediate, but deliverance is sometimes a process. We thank You for delivering us day by day from newly revealed holds that the enemy may have had on us. We stand in boldness and without fear in our deliverance, and we decree and declare that holiness and righteousness is the only thing that lives here. We ask You to create within us a clean heart and renew in us the right spirit. Please reveal to us anything that we are doing and saying that is not like You. We will work with the Holy Spirit and ask Him to help us remove those things so we can walk in the liberty and freedom that You purchased for us on Calvary. We intend to walk in that blood-bought purchase and grow from glory to glory. We take back everything that the enemy has stolen from us, starting with our minds so they can be conformed to the mind of Jesus Christ and the Word of God.

We want to please You in every way, and to protect the freedom that we have received. We know that we are the branches and You are the Vine with the life sustaining power that we need to survive. Thank You for giving us all things that pertain to life and godliness. There is nothing that we need to which we don't have access. We take You at Your Word. Thank You for delivering us from the hands of our enemies, allowing us to serve You in holiness and righteousness without fear all the days of our lives on this earth and to live with You in heaven afterwards. We ask You for forgiveness of all of our sins, known and unknown to us. As You reveal sin to us, we will repent and turn freely with Your help from it. We stand, rely and confidently trust that You and Your Word will come through for us. We thank You for these and all things in Jesus Christ's name. Amen!

Always know that God loves you, and I do, too!

66 *God's Word...*

"...*Might serve Him without fear, In holiness and righteousness before Him all the days of our life.*"

DEVOTIONAL

Day 13

The Lord is my Shepherd!

The Lord is our Shepherd, we shall not want for any good thing. He makes sure we have everything we need. He feeds, he guides, and he shields us, so we will not have any lack. He laid down His life to redeem us and restore us back to His former promise. We belong to Christ, and we are the seed of Abraham, heirs according to the promise. We are heirs of God and co-heirs with Christ Jesus, and He will withhold no good thing back from us. The Lord has been faithful to purchase us back out of the hand of the enemy. The Lord supplies our daily bread. He gives us all things that pertain to life and godliness. The earth is the Lord's and the fullness thereof, the world and they that dwell therein (Psalms 24:1 KJV). He is our helper, our director, our shield, our guide, our intercessor, and our shelter. He is the Good Shepherd. He died that we could have life and have it more abundantly, until it overflows in surplus for us to fully enjoy and to help others.

PRAYER

Heavenly Father,

Thank You for another blessed day that You have allowed us to see. Lord, we come to You with a grateful heart, thanking You for being the good, faithful, and loyal Shepherd. You supply our every need, spiritually, physically, financially, socially, and emotionally. You are the lifter of our hearts and of our heads. No good thing do You withhold from us. Thank You that when lack tries to rear its ugly head and bring poverty with it, we can go back to the Word of God and remind ourselves of who we are and whose we are. We are the head, and not the tail; we are above only and never beneath. We are the King's kids and we are robed in righteousness and royalty with Kingdom authority. We have benefits from on high that have been left to us by You, our King and our Lord. We have angels that surround us and that harken to our voices. We speak the Word only, which invites You into our life's situations with us. We are more than conquerors through Christ Jesus who loves us.

Thank You for supplying our daily bread and letting us know that without the Word, without prayer, and without obedience, we don't stand a chance. We thank You for Your faithfulness all of our days, for Your loving kindness and tender mercies that are new every morning. We have no lack, no need, that You have not already fulfilled. We believe by faith that we receive everything, every promise that You have made and purchased on the cross for us to see. We stand and confidently trust that You and Your Word will come through for us. We thank You for these and all things in Jesus Christ's name. Amen!

Always know that God loves you, and I do, too!

"The LORD is my shepherd; I shall not want."

God's Word...

"I will praise You, O LORD, with my whole heart; I will tell of all Your marvelous works. I will be glad and rejoice in You; I will sing praise to Your name, O Most High." ~ Psalms 9:1-2 NKJV

DEVOTIONAL
Day 14

I will praise You!

As a Christian, we have to, at some point, determine within our own hearts, regardless of what goes on in us or around us, we are going to praise the Lord in advance for His deliverance. We stop and remember all the times before that He has brought us out of dangerous situations, dangerous relationships, lack of finances, lack of character, lack of integrity, or loss of direction. He turns things around for us when we turn our hearts and attention back to Him and get into the Word of God so that the Word of God can get into us. When we trust Him with our whole hearts, lean not to our understanding, and acknowledge Him in all our ways, He will direct our paths. While He works out the situation around us, He is using those same situations and circumstances to work His character and integrity in us. No experience, trial or tribulation that we go through to the glory of God is in vain, if we go through it His way. Doors begin to open up to us and ways are made in His timing. God's Word says, all things work together for the good of those that love Him and who are called according to His purpose. He brings glory out of all things that we go through when we turn them over and trust in Him to bring us through. When we go through the fire with Him, there won't even be smoke on us for a witness.

PRAYER

Heavenly Father,

Thank You for another blessed day that You have allowed us to see. This is the day that You have made and we will rejoice and be glad in it. We make a quality decision to rejoice in advance of our deliverance. We thank You for all the great things You do. We praise You for the smallest things that, without You, would cease to exist. We have so much to thank You for; if we had ten thousand tongues that would not be enough. You are the true and living God, whose main desire is to fellowship in a meaningful relationship with us. You desire to talk with us and walk with us all throughout the day and to watch over and cover us at night when we lay down to a sweet sleep. You want to be more real to us than anything natural. You are the Potter and we are the clay; mold and shape us the way You want us to be. We are surrendered and available vessels that want be used for our good and for Your glory. Teach us to love what You love and hate what You hate, to walk in righteousness and holiness. We stand and confidently trust that You and Your Word will come through for us. We thank You for these and all things in Jesus Christ's name. Amen!

Always know that God loves you, and I do, too!

"I will be glad and rejoice in You..."

"Rejoice in the Lord always. Again I will say, rejoice!"
~ Philippians 4:4 NKJV

DEVOTIONAL
Day 15

Rejoice in the Lord always!

The Word of God has instructions all throughout it for us to rejoice in Him. Before we can cast our cares upon the Lord, we must first learn to celebrate God all day long! We need to look for the good that He is doing and be full of joy in the Lord, which is our strength. To be full of something means there is no room for anything else. We are to be so full of His joy that it spills over to others. We can rejoice because the earth is the Lord's and the fullness thereof, the world and all that dwell in it. We are His children and the sheep of His pasture, and He will never withhold anything that's good from us. He gives us all things that pertain to life and godliness. We are complete in Him, with nothing lacking, missing, or broken. We are to delight and gladden ourselves in Him. He wants us to have life and have it abundantly. He tells us to dream big. Write the vision and make it plain. We are commanded to increase. We are expected to succeed because we are His seed. We are the apple of His eye, His righteous ones. Our names are written in the palms of His hands and on His heart. He loves us unconditionally with goodness and mercy that follows us all the days of our lives. His favor and goodness will surround us like a shield. We the children of God have much to rejoice about for the grace that He extends to us.

PRAYER

Heavenly Father,

We thank You for another day that we can rejoice and be glad in, a day in which we acknowledge Your sovereignty. You are Lord over everything. We thank You that we are Your children and the sheep of Your pasture and that You are our good Shepherd. You supply all our needs according to your riches in glory through Christ Jesus. We rejoice in You today and celebrate all the great things that You are doing. We look for the good in every situation, for You are the Lord of the Harvest. Nothing that we go through is in vain. If we don't get the blessing, we will get the lesson and we will give You the glory.

We thank You for giving us all things richly to enjoy. When we look at all the beautiful things and places You have created, it fills our hearts with awe and amazement. We are grateful for Your loving ways that encourage, inspire, and motivate us to be obedient to the Word. We rejoice for Your healing that makes us proclaim that we will live and not die, and declare the works of the Lord. We rejoice for Your peace that surpasses all understanding and keeps our hearts and minds through Christ Jesus. We rejoice in Your salvation, knowing that we will reign with You forever. We rejoice because You give us hope, an excited expectancy for every new day to see what amazing things You are going to do through and to us today. We rejoice because we have come into a partnership of obedience with You and we take You at Your Word. We expect great things every day from You. We rejoice because success, abundance and increase are the order of the Lord for our lives. We rejoice because it pleases You that we prosper. We come to You with grateful, humble hearts, rejoicing in You always, and again we will rejoice! We stand and confidently trust that You and

Your Word will come through for us. We thank You for these and all things in Jesus Christ's name. Amen!

Always know that God loves you, and I do, too!

God's Word...

"*Rejoice in the Lord always. Again I will say, rejoice!*"

"I wait for the Lord, my whole being waits, and in his word I put my hope." ~ Psalm 130:5 NIV

DEVOTIONAL

Day 16

On His Word I put my hope!

Hope is defined as "excited expectation," which we should have at all times as we spend time in His Word.

There is a song of old that comes to mind when I meditate on this scripture: "On Christ the solid Rock I stand, all other ground is sinking sand. All other ground is sinking sand." In His Word alone do we put our hope. Christ is the only Solid Rock for us to stand on that will not falter nor fail us. Thank God for all the great people in our lives, but at the end of the day, we all need God. They can't handle the pressures of being God to someone else, so don't put them in a position to disappoint and fail you. People come and people go, but God will never leave nor forsake you. We can stand on His Word, and it is more than able to sustain us. At any time, we can talk to Him and rest assured that He hears and will answer our prayers. We can put our hope in Him and wait patiently in peace, knowing He's in the background working things out for us, and we will never be ashamed. When we turn situations and circumstances over to His capable hands, He rewards those who diligently seek, trust and believe in Him. Put your confidence, trust, and hope in Him, who alone lovingly created this whole beautiful world for you to have a place to thrive, live in and enjoy.

PRAYER

Heavenly Father,

Thank You for another day to give You glory, honor, and praise. Thank You for allowing us the opportunity to come boldly before the Throne of Grace, to present to You our concerns and cares. You said in Your Word that we could cast our cares on You, for You care for us. We wait patiently for You, Lord, when we are sick for the healing from the Balm of Gilead and from the Great Physician. We wait when our finances are low for You to make provisions, open doors, give favor, and make ways for us. We wait when our minds are overwhelmed for the peace that surpasses all understanding and for clarity that can only come from You. We wait for Your unconditional love to shower us when we don't know how to truly love ourselves. We openly and unashamedly acknowledge that we can do nothing and will not try to without You. We wait for You, Lord. Our whole being waits, and in Your Word do we put our hope. We stand, rely and confidently trust that You and Your Word will come through for us. We thank You for these and all things in Jesus Christ's name. Amen!

Always know that God loves you, and I do, too!

"God's Word..." *"I wait for the Lord, my whole being waits, and in his word I put my hope."*

"Behold, I will do a new thing, Now it shall spring forth; Shall you not know it? I will even make a road in the wilderness and rivers in the desert." ~ Isaiah 43:19 NKJV

DEVOTIONAL

Day 17

God is doing a new thing!

As children of the Most High, we should always be expecting the unexpected, for God is always doing a new thing. Your situation can change at any time for He is also God of the reversal. He is the creator of everything. Who else can make a road in the wilderness and a river in the desert? He is always looking for ways to bless us and to show Himself strong in the midst of everything. His ears are open to our cry and He knows all that's in our hearts. His Word has the answer to every problem because He is the problem solver. He has placed us in authority to speak to a thing, and cause it to be as we said. We serve a mighty God, whose desire is always to do good towards us. He wants us to walk by faith and not by sight, and He is still doing miracles. He is the only one in the position to do anything but fail, if we would only believe.

PRAYER

Heavenly Father,

Thank You for blessing us with another day. Our expectations are high to see Your miracle-working power. We look for all the good things that You have planned for us, and we praise You for them in advance. You are a "suddenly" God, who can make things spring forth. Help us to recognize when You are at work because opportunity is often disguised as opposition. Help us to stand on your Word, which keeps us stable and consistent. Help us not to be weary in well doing, because we know we shall reap if we will not faint. You are the rock of our salvation. You are our way maker. You are the provider of every good thing. You are the one who can put joy in our hearts and make our hearts sing. You are Lord of the open doors, and You are doing a new thing for us. Our hope and excited expectation of Your loving kindness and tender mercies follow us forever. We thank You for who You are, the King of kings and Lord of lords. You are the Lord of the Harvest and we sow seeds toward our promised land. We live the sweet life, in the land of milk and honey. We thank You for making a road in the wilderness and rivers in the desert. We stand and confidently trust that You and Your Word will come through for us. We thank You for these and all things in Jesus Christ's name. Amen!

Always know that God loves you, and I do, too!

> God's Word...
>
> *"Behold, I will do a new thing, Now it shall spring forth."*

"He restores my soul; He leads me in the paths of righteousness For His name's sake." ~ Psalms 23:3 NKJV

DEVOTIONAL
Day 18

The Good Shepherd restores!

As our Good Shepherd, God is the only one who can restore our souls, which are made up of our minds, wills, and emotions. He restores us physically with overflowing healing, from the crowns of our heads to the soles of feet. He is also able to restore us emotionally. He is the lifter of our hearts and our heads. He makes us strong so we can turn around and help others. Finally, He restores us financially so that we can further the Gospel, and so that the needs of His people will be met.

God offers restoration and rejuvenation to us as His children. We are the apple of God's eye; we are His beloved, we are complete in Christ Jesus, and we stand in His righteousness. This means that we can come boldly before the throne of grace to receive help in a time of need. Whatever we stand in need of, the Lord stands ready to share it with us. He leads us in the path of righteousness for His name's sake, and our job is to give Him glory for all that He does. We ought not look to the left or to the right but straight ahead to the Lord. God cleanses our hearts and our hands, and as we put on the new man, we have to remember that holiness is always the order of God, and He rewards that. We no longer habitually sin, but we walk in integrity, holiness, and righteousness. We live a life set apart to give glory to God for His name's sake.

PRAYER

Heavenly Father,

Thank You for another blessed day that You have allowed us to see. We ask that You cover us and our family members, friends, and those who don't know You in the pardoning of their sin. We thank You for being a holy God, and for creating within us clean hearts and right spirits. We thank You for setting us apart and sanctifying us for the furtherance of Your kingdom. There is peace in our hearts when we walk according to Your Word. There is joy unspeakable that You give to us. Consuming fire of God, burn out anything in us that is not of You. Holiness is still the right way if we want to see Your power manifested boldly in us today. You said when a man's or woman's ways please You, You make his enemies to be at peace with him.

Thank You for leading us in the path of righteousness for Your name's sake. You are our Savior and Lord, and all that we say and do should be to bring glory to You. We thank You because You are the soon coming King, and we want to live a life now with power, authority, and victory so we can continue to reign with You when You come again. We give You glory, honor, and praise, and we bless Your holy and righteous name. We stand and confidently trust that You and Your Word will come through for us. We thank You for these and all things in Jesus Christ's name. Amen!

Always know that God loves you, and I do, too!

God's Word...   *"He restores my soul…"*

"But let all those rejoice who put their trust in You; Let them ever shout for joy, because You defend them; Let those also who love Your name Be joyful in You." ~ Psalms 5:11 NKJV

DEVOTIONAL

Day 19

Be joyful in the Lord!

The children of the Lord can rejoice when we put our trust in Him. We can shout for joy, because He will defend us no matter what. No matter the battle, it is already won when we make Jesus Christ our Lord and Savior. We fight from a place of victory, which is why rejoicing is the order that we receive. When we belong to the Lord, we come on the winning side every day of our lives. Our victory is stacked in the favor of God, who surrounds us like a shield. No weapon formed against us will prosper, and any tongue that rises against us is already condemned. We send each and every one of them back to the sender. We are joyful because we love God, and we know that His powerful and majestic name is above every situation, circumstance, or obstacle that we will ever face. We know we have everything we stand in need of and we are joyful, because He is the great, powerful and generous Lord of the Harvest.

PRAYER

Heavenly Father,

Thank You for another blessed day that You have allowed us to see. Hallelujah to the Lord of lords and King of kings. Because we put our trust in You, we know we win. You are the Lord of the Harvest. You know all things that we are presented with, and You have the answer to each and every one of them. We thank You and rejoice in You today because the Holy Spirit within us reveals the secret things we need to know. He directs our paths with instructions and strategies to succeed. Your joy, Lord, is our strength. You fill us with Your joy for the task at hand. You fill us with Your peace, which surpasses all understanding and keeps our hearts and minds in Christ Jesus. You comfort the grieving heart, for Your Word says that those who mourn will be comforted. You restore our souls and broken relationships. You heal sickness and disease, and raise us up from our deathbeds. You defend us from our enemies, and set a table before them where they have to watch us succeed. You provide everything we have need of, and surround us with favor like a shield. We are always in the right place, at the right time, saying and doing the right thing for divine connections to our destiny for our good and for Your glory. We are thankful to You, Lord, for all the great things You have done and that You are doing. We can rejoice today because we belong to You, and You are the good, good Father. We stand and confidently trust that You and Your Word will come through for us. We thank You for these and all things in Jesus Christ's name. Amen!

Always know that God loves you, and I do, too!

God's Word...

"Let those also who love Your name be joyful in You."

"For You, O LORD, will bless the righteous; With favor You will sur-round him as with a shield." ~ Psalms 5:12 NKJV

DEVOTIONAL
Day 20

The righteous are shielded with favor!

No matter where you are in life, always remember that if you are a righteous child of the true and living God, your victory is found in His favor. Everywhere you turn, He reveals His favor. The Lord's anger will last for a moment, but His favor lasts a lifetime. Weeping may stay for the night, but rejoicing comes in the morning. The Lord God is a sun that lights the way and a shield that protects you day by day. No good thing does He withhold from those whose walk is blameless. When a man's ways please the Lord, He makes even His enemies to be at peace with him. The Lord will come to your aid and save you when you cry out to Him, trusting and believing in Him. The Lord will send helpers that you need to get to your destiny. He will open doors and make ways for you to get to your next assignment. He will strengthen your weak places and cleanse you from all unrighteousness when it's confessed to Him. The Lord blesses the righteous with favor and surrounds him as with a shield.

PRAYER

Heavenly Father,

Thank You for another blessed day that You have allowed us to see. Lord, we remember that Your favor rests on us. It establishes the work of our hands. We thank You that it's Your grace and unmerited favor that sustain our lives each and every day. Lord, You know all things and You guide us into our wealthy place with Your favor. As we meditate on Your Word day and night, the Word is where we get our direction, our marching orders, our instructions for daily living. In Your favor we find healing, strength, comfort, joy, peace, forgiveness and anything else that we will ever need. Thank You for giving us all things that pertain to life and godliness. Thank You for Your favor that surrounds us as a shield. We look to You only for our every need to be met. Lord, help us to remember at all times that our victory is found in Your favor. We stand and confidently trust that You and Your Word will come through for us. We thank You for these and all things in Jesus Christ's name. Amen!

Always know that God loves you, and I do, too!

" God's Word... "With favor You will surround him as with a shield."

"Who has believed our report? And to whom has the arm of the LORD been revealed?" ~ Isaiah 53:1 NKJV

Day 21

Whose report will you believe?

We have multiple opportunities throughout the day to decide whose report we will believe. Will it be the Word of God or the world's report? The decision that we make will determine the outcome of our situation, be it supernatural or natural. The world's ways are limited in every way but the Word of God is unlimited and unstoppable when we truly believe it. The Arm of the Lord will be revealed to those who confidently trust, adhere to and rely on Him. He will show Himself strong with infinite power and a mighty hand to those who trust and believe in Him. No foe or enemy can stand against the all-knowing, ever-present, all-powerful true and living God's children. That includes sickness, pain, guilt, shame, confusion, grief, addictions, and defeat.

We stand in awe of the Almighty God who is our Father. We battle from a place of victory to hold on to what has already been purchased for us on Calvary. We don't have to wait until the battle is over, we can shout now. We know that we are more than conquerors, we are world over-comers, we walk in freedom and liberty, and it's all through Christ Jesus. We choose to believe the report of Lord, which only brings good things to us with no negative side effects to them.

PRAYER

Heavenly Father,

Thank You for another blessed day that You have allowed us to see. We thank You for the unadulterated Word of God that cannot be manipulated or destroyed. The Word of God's report is the anchor we stand on to keep us stable in the middle of storms. We know Your Word is everlasting and will not return to You void, and You watch over us day and night to perform and bring it to pass for us. Thank You for Your unconditional, unrelenting, everlasting love that covers us at all times. We thank You for You being the Great I Am, the Great Physician, the Alpha and Omega, and the True and Living God who takes care of us morning, noon, and night. We stand in awe of You and appreciate all that You do. We have made a quality decision within our hearts that we will believe the report of the Lord throughout all situations, obstacles, and circumstances. We stand and confidently trust that You and Your Word will come through for us. We thank You for these and all things in Jesus Christ's name. Amen!

Always know that God loves you, and I do, too!

God's Word...

"*And to whom has the arm of the LORD been revealed.*"

"I sought the LORD, and He heard me, And delivered me from all my fears." ~ Psalms 34:4 NKJV

DEVOTIONAL
Day 22

The Lord heard my cry!

Every parent knows the individual cry of each of their children's voices, and it gets their immediate attention so that they come running at the sound of it. The Lord is the same way with each one of us. When we sincerely cry out to the Lord with all of our hearts for help that only He can give us, He hears the words that come out of our mouths and He delivers us from all of our fears. He reminds us that He has not given us a spirit of fear, but of power, love, and a sound mind. The victory belongs to Jesus, and deliverance belongs to us. He is always working in the background to help us to walk in wholeness and completeness, for we are complete in Christ Jesus.

His unconditional love always shows up to strengthen us where we are weak and build us up where we are torn down. The Lord is stronger than any fear that we can encounter. He has placed the same strength in us. The joy of the Lord is our strength. As we thank Him for what He has already done in the past, and for working behind the scenes for us in the present, His strength will rise up on the inside of us from the joy of thanksgiving and appreciation. We can pour our hearts out to the Lord, but we always have to end our prayers with what the Word says about our situation. We always pray the solution, not the problem. The Lord moves in response according to His promises, and the angels hearken so they can bring to pass what we speak into the atmosphere by faith. That is why we can trust in the Lord alone to deliver us and not in our situations or people for our answers.

PRAYER

Heavenly Father,

Thank You for another blessed day that You have allowed us to see. We thank You for being all present, all powerful, and all knowing! Thank You for being attentive to our cry and for listening for Your Words in order to perform them. You said Your Word will not return to You void, so we say what You say in agreement with You. We stand on Your Word and wait on You to perform it with joy and hope, with an excited expectation and anticipation. You are a true and living God. You are a mighty and powerful miracle worker. We say we are healed by Your stripes, we are strengthened by Your might, we are covered in Your blood, and we are protected by Your angels.

We extend our hope and trust in You, knowing You are the only one who can deliver us from ourselves, and from others. There is nothing too hard for You, Lord. You are beautiful for every situation that we find ourselves in. You supply seed to the sower, and bread for food. You multiply the seed we have sown and increase the fruits of our righteousness, while we are enriched in everything for all liberality, causing a heart of thanksgiving directed to You. We plant the seed of Your Word into our hearts by mediating on it day and night. We give You time for the seed to grow, then we reap the harvest at Your appointed time for us. We give You all the glory, all the honor, and all the praise for all the great and mighty things that You have done and that You are doing for us daily. We stand and confidently trust that You and Your Word will come through for us. We thank You for these and all things in Jesus Christ's name. Amen!

Always know that God loves you, and I do, too!

God's Word...

"I sought the LORD, and He heard me..."

Therefore purge out the old leaven, that you may be a new lump, since you truly are unleavened. For indeed Christ, our Passover, was sacrificed for us. Therefore let us keep the feast, not with old leaven, nor with the leaven of malice and wickedness, but with the unleavened bread of sincerity and truth." ~ I Corinthians 5:7-8 NKJV

DEVOTIONAL
Day 23

Remember the Sacrifice!

When we remember the ones who lost their lives in loving sacrifice in the four levels of armed forces for our protection and freedom, we say "thank you" for their sacrifice and we pray for their family members. In a similar way, Jesus Christ, our Passover sacrifice, allows us to live a life of ultimate freedom from sin and death, with liberty to enjoy His love, deliverance, forgiveness, goodness and mercy that's renewed every morning for us. Jesus made what is called a freewill sacrifice, which is the surrender or destruction of something desirable for the sake of something considered as having a higher or more pressing claim. This incomparable gift lets us live a life in which we can walk away from darkness and put away malice (ill will, hate, bitterness, spiteful behavior) and wickedness (evil, iniquity, dishonesty, perversion), and take up a life of walking in the light of sincerity and truth.

Therefore, we show we appreciate the sacrifice that He made for us by making similar efforts to sacrifice our lives to show the love of Jesus Christ and help others come into the knowledge of Him and be saved.

PRAYER

Heavenly Father,

Thank You for another blessed day that You have allowed us to see. Thank You for the living sacrifice that Jesus Christ, our Passover Lamb, made for us. It was His willing sacrifice of His life that allows us to be saved, delivered, and set free so we can spend eternity with You. We thank You for Your everlasting love that relentlessly comes after us and never gives up. We thank You for Your many precious promises that are 'Yes' and 'Amen' (so be it). We thank You for Your favor that surrounds us like a shield. We thank You for instructing us and teaching us the way we should go and for guiding us with Your eyes. You are the everlasting, Good Father that comforts us when we mourn. Thank You for healing our hearts and filling every void in our lives with Your unconditional love. Thank You for the gift of The Blessing. Thank You that we are always in the right place at the right time, doing and saying the right thing for divine connections for our good and for Your glory. We give You glory, honor and praise for the ultimate sacrifice and for taking such good care of us who belong to You. We stand and confidently trust that You and Your Word will come through for us. We thank You for these and all things in Jesus Christ's name. Amen!

Always know that God loves you, and I do, too!

God's Word... "For indeed Christ, our Passover, was sacrificed for us."

"I will love You, O LORD, my strength. The LORD is my rock and my fortress and my deliverer; My God, my strength, in whom I will trust; My shield and the horn of my salvation, my stronghold." ~ Psalms 18:1-2 NKJV

DEVOTIONAL
Day 24

The Lord is my Rock! The Lord is my everything!

When you've gone through some things with God and He has shown His loyalty, His faithfulness, and His unlimited power, you will cry out with a sincere heart, "I will love you, O Lord, my strength." You will know that without Him, you could not have made it. When you are a child of God, you never have to feel like you are alone for He has said He will never leave nor forsake you. He is the lifter of our heads when we need encouragement. He is the lover of our souls and our quick defense. Anytime you feel like you cannot go on, think of who you belong to and know He has no limits. There is no situation too hard for God, nor does He stand in a corner scratching His head trying to figure things out. He is the all-knowing, all-powerful, ever-present God. You can't get up early enough to catch Him off guard, because He NEVER sleeps nor slumbers.

When you become a child of God, you develop a relationship with Jesus Christ and have the Holy Spirit deposited into you. Once that happens, there is nothing through Jesus Christ that you can't do. The same power that raised Jesus Christ from the dead now lives in you. You are empowered with everything in life that you will ever need when you join in a covenant with the Trinity. God is our strength in whom we can trust and take refuge. He is our shield and buckler; He shields the blows that the enemy throws in an effort to destroy. He is our shield of protection from danger everywhere we go. He is the horn of our salvation with potency and power, our stronghold and high tower. When you realize that God is all you've got, you'll see that God is all you need.

PRAYER

Heavenly Father,

Thank You for another blessed day that You have allowed us to see. Lord, You are everything!

Everything we have need of, You provide for us. You answer us before we call. You are the Sovereign Lord. You work behind the scenes setting situations up for us. Sometimes things look like they are going wrong, but You said that all things work together for the good for those who love You and who are called according to Your purpose. We are called, anointed, and appointed with a purpose for You. Thank You God for teaching us that we walk by faith and not by sight, knowing that, no matter what happens to us, we will come out on top. You are our all in all. You are always with us through every one of life's encounters. Thank You for goodness and mercy that follows us all the days of our lives. Thank You for Your favor that surrounds us like a shield. Thank You for the peace that surpasses all understanding. You are a miracle working God. Thank You for healing, deliverance, protection, provision, abundance, and for allowing us to be a distribution center for You. We love You, O Lord, our strength and our redeemer. We stand and confidently trust that You and Your Word will come through for us. We thank You for these and all things in Jesus Christ's name. Amen!

Always know that God loves you, and I do, too!

God's Word... "The LORD is my rock and my fortress and my deliverer."

"And raised us up together, and made us sit together in the heavenly places in Christ Jesus…" ~ *Ephesians 2:6 NKJV*

Day 25

Location, Location, Location!

My brother is a realtor and when I was looking for a house, he said that in real estate, everything is about location. The value of a house is often determined by the location of the property. The better the location, the higher the price, and the better the features are in the house. My question now is, where are you located in Christ Jesus? There are not qualities greater than what He places on the inside of those who belong to Him, but you determine what location you are going to live in. Are you in heavenly places, flying and soaring like the eagles, high above and over situations, problems, and circumstances? Or, are you sitting below with the chickens pecking on the ground with natural remedies and following the system of the world? Are you speaking the Word of God against the circumstances that are trying to bombard you? Are you telling the situations what the Word says and commanding them to line up with it? Are you keeping your eyes, heart, and mind stayed on Christ Jesus day and night so that you will make your own way prosperous and have success? The Lord already knows the problems; we only have to speak the solutions. We have to keep looking up to the hills where our help comes from and never stop looking in that direction.

PRAYER

Heavenly Father,

Thank You for another blessed day that You have allowed us to see. We thank You that we know our location, and for a high position seated in heavenly places in Christ Jesus. We remind ourselves that we are to always behave as though that's where we are. When we say what You say, we will have what You want us to have. We are the head only and not the tail, above only and not beneath. We are accepted in the Beloved already. We are the righteousness of God in Christ Jesus. We are more than conquerors through Christ who loves us. We fight from a place of victory. We are world overcomers in Christ Jesus. We are ambassadors for Christ, the light of the world. We are saved by grace. We are born of incorruptible seed. We are forgiven of all our sins. We are part of the royal priesthood. We are a chosen generation. We are a citizen of the kingdom of heaven. We are joint heirs with Jesus. We are complete in Him. We are crucified with Christ. We are alive with Christ. We are first and not last. We are strong in You and in the power of Your might. We have a spirit of power, love, and a sound mind. We are healed by Jesus' stripes. We are comforted by The Holy Spirit. We are called by You. We are fearfully and wonderfully made. We are partakers of Your divine nature. We are the apple of Your eye. We are changed into Your image. We soar like the eagles.

Thank You, Jesus, for many great and precious promises. We ask You to help us grab hold every day and not let go until we see what we say in agreement with You. We stand and confidently trust that You and Your Word will come through for us. We thank You for these and all things in Jesus Christ's name. Amen!

Always know that God loves you, and I do, too!

God's Word... *"And raised us up together..."*

"But the LORD said to Samuel, 'Do not look at his appearance or at his physical stature, because I have refused him. For the LORD does not see as man sees; for man looks at the outward appearance, but the LORD looks at the heart.'" ~ I Samuel 16:7 NKJV

DEVOTIONAL
Day 26

It's a heart thing!

I was passing by a house the other day that was a new construction, and the sign out front read, "Starting at the 200's." Before I knew it, I said aloud, "Who's going to pay that much for those houses since they are built so close together? They must have some mighty good amenities on the inside of them to put that price on it." Then the Lord spoke to my spirit and said, "That's how it is with us. To other people, we don't always look on the outside like the value we carry on the inside." That's why He said man looks on the outside, but He looks on the heart. It's an inside job, and the heart makes all the difference. Jesus sees value in us when the outside is still acting up. He knows that once He deposits His heart on the inside of us, if we surrender and follow Him, in time all of our features will change for the better. The more quality time we spend with Him in surrender, the more the Holy Spirit can transform our lives into a usable vessel. We can have a heart to carry the glory of God with love, power, and authority. We become the ambassadors of Christ Jesus, the agents of change for the world that He always intended for us to be. Out of the abundance of the heart, the mouth speaks. Whatever is in your heart is what is eventually going to come out. We want to speak good things so we will have a good life and God will be glorified.

PRAYER

Heavenly Father,

Thank You for another blessed day that You have allowed us to see. We thank You for revealing to us that it is the heart of a man or woman that makes them who they are. You said that as a man thinks in His heart, so is He. What we are meditating on is very important for it determines what we become. Lord, help us to understand that whatever we look at on a constant basis is what we will conform to. Life is to be enjoyed and not just endured, and we determine which one we will do by our own words. Let the words of our mouths and the meditation of our hearts be acceptable in Your sight, oh Lord, our strength and our redeemer. Help us meditate on Your Words day and night, so we will observe and do them. Then, You said, we will make our own way prosper and succeed. It's Your Word in our hearts, spoken out of our mouths in trust and belief in the Word's merit alone that will bring us transformation, rejuvenation, and our excited expectations of a SUDDENLY manifestation from the spirit to the natural.

Lord, You said above all else for us to guard our hearts for out of them flow the issues of life. You tell us not to harden our hearts when we hear Your voice. You tell us that a happy heart makes the face merry, but sorrow crushes the spirit. Everything starts with the heart, then it branches out into every other area of our lives. We ask that You create in us a clean heart and renew the right spirit in us. Help us to walk upright before You and treasure only You, for You said where our treasure is, there our hearts will be also. Help us to hide the Word in our hearts that we might not sin against You. Then our minds will be regulated, our hearts will be changed, and manifestations will come quicker. We stand, rely and confidently trust that You and Your Word will come through for us. We thank You for these and all things in Jesus Christ's name. Amen!

Always know that God loves you, and I do, too!

God's Word... " . . . for man looks at the outward appearance, but the LORD looks at the heart."

"Casting down arguments and every high thing that exalts itself against the knowledge of God, bringing every thought into captivity to the obedience of Christ..." ~ *II Corinthians 10:5 NKJV*

DEVOTIONAL
Day 27

*C*ast down arguments and every high thing!

We are at war and the battlefield is in our mind. We have to take every thought captive that is contrary to the Word of God. Since we have been raised up with Christ at the new birth, we seek things above, where Christ is, and not things below, where we are. We use our sword, which is the Word of God, to destroy any and every high thing that exalts itself against the knowledge of God and we bring it captive into obedience to Christ Jesus. We are commanded to study to show ourselves approved, a workman that need not be ashamed, rightly dividing the Word of Truth (II Timothy 2:15). The truth is that the enemy put thoughts into our minds. Those thoughts when meditated on produce strongholds, which produce feelings, which left unchecked lead us into bondage. We must cast down arguments in our minds, and then we must replace them with what the Word of God says about them. We call on the power twins, faith and hope (excited expectations in anticipation), to help us to stand firm, hold fast and win in every arena.

The answer to every problem in life is written in the Word of God. We have not been left to defend for ourselves. We have a good shepherd and savior who is our defense, who, by the Holy Spirit, leads and guides us into all truth. We have to come into agreement with Him and say only what He says. We are commanded not to be conformed to the patterns of this world, but be transformed by the renewing our mind by the Word of God. We have the victory in Christ Jesus when we meditate on the Word day and night as He has instructed us.

PRAYER

Heavenly Father,

Thank You for another blessed day that You have allowed us to see. Help us to keep our minds on You and be intentional about what we allow to filter through it. Help us to think on whatever things are true, whatever things are noble, whatever things are just, whatever things are pure, whatever things are lovely, and whatever things are of good report. If there is any virtue and if there is anything praiseworthy, help us to meditate on these things (Philippians 4:8). You said, You would keep us in perfect peace if we keep our minds on You because we trust in You. You are the great and mighty, true and living God, and there is no one to compare to You. You and the Word are One. We thank You that we can stand on, trust, rely, and abide in the Word and it will never let us fall, nor will it forsake us. Thank You that You are strong enough to hold the whole world intact, and gentle enough to hold us and all that concerns us safely in it. We thank You that the Word of God is faithful, strong, loyal, and true, and we have everything we need in us to do what you've instructed us to do. We stand and confidently trust that You and Your Word will come through for us. We thank You for these and all things in Jesus Christ's name. Amen!

Always know that God loves you, and I do, too!

God's Word... "...*bringing every thought into captivity to the obedience of Christ.*"

"For all the promises of God in Him are Yes, and in Him Amen, to the glory of God through us." ~ II Corinthians 1:20 NKJV

DEVOTIONAL
Day 28

*Y*es and Amen to all of the promises!

We serve a great, loving, kind, wonderful, fantastic and magnificent God who said that all of the promises in Him are Yes, and in Him Amen. First we have to be in Him in order for the promises to work through us. Then we have to find a promise in His Word and place pressure on the scripture by sticking with it, using the measure of faith that we have, and knowing that God's Word will not return unto Him void. It will accomplish what He pleases. He will fulfill the Word that we stand on unwaveringly; it is His heart's desire toward us. It has always been His intention to be good to us, to heal us from all sickness and disease, and to deliver us from all of our enemies. His desire is to restore the joy of our salvation, to give strength to the weary and give power to the weak, and to save us along with our household.

We combine faith with hope and an excited anticipation of the expectation of the manifestation of the promise. Since we stand on His Word, we ought not speak contrary to it. We will not abort our harvest by speaking ill about it in the middle of its manifestation. We should speak life at all times, as we meditate on His Word of Promise day and night, and we will make our way prosperous and have good success. We will walk, talk, and agree with the unadulterated Word of God, that has all power and hope in it that we will ever need to experience every victory in life.

PRAYER

Heavenly Father,

Thank You for another blessed day that You have allowed us to see. We bless Your holy and righteous name because all the promises of God in Him are Yes, and in Him Amen! Thank You that once we have accepted Jesus as Lord and Savior of our lives, we are now in Him. Now we qualify for the 'Yes' and 'Amen'. We are privileged to have an opportunity daily to partner with You, to walk in agreement with Your Word, trusting You to bring to pass what You have already ordained for us. We know that Your Word will not return to You void, but it will accomplish what You have sent it to do. As ambassadors of Jesus Christ, we speak the Word or decree a thing and it will come to pass. We thank You for the plans that You have to prosper us and not to harm us, plans to give us hope and a future.

Thank You that You are not a man that You should lie, nor the son of man that You should repent. Thank You that You said in Your Word that heaven and earth would fade away, but Your Word in no wise will pass away. We have assurance that we can stand on the promises of Your Word and they will come to pass, as long as we hold on to them. We walk by faith and not by sight. We see the end from the beginning with our imagination as You did when You created us. We expect goodness and mercy to follow us all the days of our lives; we expect to have favor with God and man; we expect to be crowned daily with Your loving-kindness and tender mercies. We thank You that it's Your desire to give us all that we expect, only when we find that promise in Your Word. We give You glory, honor, and praise for all the great things You constantly do for us. We stand and confidently trust that You and Your Word will come through for us. We thank You for these and all things in Jesus Christ's name. Amen!

Always know that God loves you, and I do, too!

God's Word...

"For all the promises of God in Him are Yes, and in Him Amen."

"For You, LORD, are most high above all the earth; You are exalted far above all gods." ~ Psalms 97:9 NKJV

DEVOTIONAL
Day 29

G od is exalted far above all gods!

Some people have many gods and don't even know it. If you spend more time washing your car, working on a job, rearing your children, or loving your wife or husband, and it's not being done for the glory of God, I have one question: have you created a god out of what or who He has given you? God is above everything and everyone; without Him nothing exists. He is The One who gave us everything and everyone we have. He gives us life-sustaining breath each day to breathe, and He regulates the beat of our hearts and of all internal organs. He gives us movement from one place to another. He gives everything that pertains to life and godliness. Our hearts should be full of praise and adoration for all the wonderful blessings He bestows upon us each day. He is our rock in a weary land. He is our hope in every situation. He is our strength in the middle of a storm. He is our comforter when our hearts are broken. He is our healer from all sickness and diseases. He is our provider for every need. He is our defense when we are done wrong, and He is our shield from every fiery dart. There is no other than we can depend on and who is with us 24/7. We will exalt nothing or no one above our God.

PRAYER

Heavenly Father,

Thank You for another blessed day that You have allowed us to see. This is the day that You have made, and we will rejoice and be glad in it. We thank You for Your loving kindness and tender mercies that grace us this day with life. We come to You with a grateful heart and a teachable spirit. We are open and willing vessels for Your mission. Let Your kingdom come and Your will be done in our lives as we exalt You far above all gods. You are the Great I AM, the All Sustaining One, the Ancient of Days, the author and finisher of our faith. You are Jehovah Yireh, our Provider; Jehovah Rapha, our Healer; Jehovah Niss'i , our Banner; Jehovah Shalom, our Peace; and Jehovah Ra-ah, You are the Way, our Shepherd. There is no need that we have on this earth that You have not already fulfilled. We give You glory, honor, and praise. To the only wise God, our Savior, be glory, majesty, dominion, authority and power both now and forevermore (Jude 1:25, KJV). We will never cease to give You praise as our spirits rejoice in God our Savior. We stand and confidently trust that You and Your Word will come through for us. We thank You for these and all things in Jesus Christ's name. Amen!

Always know that God loves you, and I do, too!

God's Word...

"For you are exalted far above all gods."

"Blessed is the man Who walks not in the counsel of the ungodly, Nor stands in the path of sinners, Nor sits in the seat of the scornful; But his delight is in the law of the LORD, And in His law he meditates day and night. He shall be like a tree Planted by the rivers of water, That brings forth its fruit in its season, Whose leaf also shall not wither; And whatever he does shall prosper." ~ Psalms 1:1-3 NKJV

DEVOTIONAL
Day 30

To be Blessed!

The Lord gives specific instructions that if you want to be blessed, do not walk in the counsel of the ungodly. Don't follow their advice and expect good to come from it, and don't stand (be submissive and inactive) in the path where sinners walk. He warns us not to sit down where the scornful gather. Instead, our delight and desire is to be in the law of the Lord, and on His law (precepts, instructions, teachings) we should habitually meditate (ponder and study) by day and by night. Our lives are saturated with the Word of God. The Word and our obedience to it is the foundation and basis for our prosperity and success in life. We will prosper in our season as long as we walk, talk, live, and breathe the Word of God. Consistency in the Word of God is the key to partaking of all that the Lord purchased for us on Calvary. Looking to the Holy Spirit, our helper, for guidance, we acknowledge Him before anything we do to make sure we are going in the right direction, and whatever we do will prosper and succeed in the proper season.

PRAYER

Heavenly Father,

Thank You for another blessed day that You have allowed us to see. We thank You for the precious Holy Spirit and the precious Word of God. Thank You for teaching us Your ways and instructing us day by day in the righteous path that you planned for us, around the traps, pitfalls, plots, and plans that the enemy has set. We thank You that You are the all wise God and that You love us unconditionally. Your desire is for us to prosper in everything we put our hands to. Thank You for letting us know that outside of the Word of God, there will be temporary and very limited prosperity. Thank You for letting us sit at Your feet, learning of You, studying and meditating on Your Word so that it flows freely from the root of the vine to us, Your branches. This is Your form of communication, and our sustaining hope and grace. We don't take for granted the opportunity to speak the Word consistently and watch it do the work along with our faith in You, and with the Holy Spirit's instructions. We are Bible believing, walk on the water, victorious, more than conqueror men and women of God. We walk by faith and not by sight. We stand in awe of Your glory and power. We stand and confidently trust that You and Your Word will come through for us. We thank You for these and all things in Jesus Christ's name. Amen!

Always know that God loves you, and I do, too!

God's Word... "And whatever he does shall prosper."

"Bless the LORD, O my soul; And all that is within me, bless His holy name! Bless the LORD, O my soul, And forget not all His benefits."
~ Psalms 103:1-2 NKJV

DEVOTIONAL
Day 31

The Lord has benefits!

Most jobs that you're on have benefits of one kind or another. In the same way, the Lord has benefits that He gives when you love and serve Him. He tells us in Psalms 103 not to forget any of the benefits He gives. He forgives all of our iniquities (immoral or grossly unfair behavior, sinful nature). He heals all our diseases. He redeems our lives from destruction. He beautifies, dignifies and crowns us with loving kindness and tender mercies. He satisfies (meets the expectations, needs, or desires of) our mouth with good things, so that our youth is renewed like the eagles'. The Lord executes righteousness and judgment for all that are oppressed. He made known His ways unto Moses, His acts unto the children of Israel. The Lord is merciful and gracious, slow to anger, and plenteous in mercy and loving kindness. He will not always chide (scold or rebuke); neither will He keep His anger forever or hold a grudge. He has not dealt with us after our sins or rewarded us according to our iniquities, for as the heavens are high above the earth, so great is His mercy toward those who reverently and worshipfully fear Him. As a father loves and pities his children, so the Lord loves and pities those who fear Him. The mercy and loving kindness of the Lord are from everlasting to everlasting for those who reverently fear Him, and His righteousness is to His children's children.

PRAYER

Heavenly Father,

Thank You for another blessed day that You have allowed us to see. We thank You for all of Your benefits. You are the giver, but You're under no obligation to give. It's strictly out of Your everlasting and unconditional love for us. It is that love that seals us with Your precious Holy Spirit, that forgives us from all of our sins, and that heals us from all diseases. It saves us from destruction, corruption, and the pit. Your love does not deal with us according to our sins nor rewards us according to our iniquities. It's Your loving kindness and tender mercies that remembers that we are dust and has pity on us. We ask You to create in us a clean heart and renew a right spirit, so we might keep Your commandments and not sin against You. Thank You for helping us to keep Your covenant, which will allow You to give mercy and righteousness to our children's children. We ask You to help us always to have a soft heart, kind words and a loving demeanor which only comes from spending time in the loving presence and power of our Heavenly Father. We stand in awe of all of the benefits that You freely give to us, and we humbly bow within our hearts and say we love You and thank You. We stand and confidently trust that You and Your Word will come through for us. We thank You for these and all things in Jesus Christ's name. Amen!

Always know that God loves you, and I do, too!

God's Word...

"Bless the LORD, O my soul."

My Prayer For You!

May this labor of love
Be a blessing to your
spirit, heart, and soul.
May you dwell in
The Lord's presence
And continue to grow.
May you be assured that
He is faithful and true, and
that He will never leave
nor forsake you.
May you understand his desire
For a personal and intimate relationship with you, and
May you always know
That The Lord unconditionally, relentlessly, and affectionately
loves you, and I do too!

From My Heart to Yours!
By: Yvonne D. Quarles

CPSIA information can be obtained
at www.ICGtesting.com
Printed in the USA
JSHW011722261219
3201JS00004B/13